ADAPTED FOR SUCCESS

POISON FROGS
AND OTHER AMPHIBIANS

Andrew Solway

Heinemann Library
Chicago, Illinois

Customer Service   888–454–2279

Visit our website at www.heinemannlibrary.com

Photo research by Mica Brancic and Susi Paz
Designed by Richard Parker
Printed and bound in China by WKT Company Ltd

11 10 09 08 07
10 9 8 7 6 5 4 3 2 1

Library of Congress Cataloging-in-Publication Data
Solway, Andrew.
  Poison frogs and other amphibians / Andrew Solway.
    p. cm. -- (Adapted for success)
  Includes bibliographical references and index.
  ISBN-13: 978-1-4034-8225-9 (library binding (hardcover))
  ISBN-10: 1-4034-8225-X
  ISBN-13: 978-1-4034-8232-7 (pbk.)
  ISBN-10: 1-4034-8232-2
  1. Dendrobatidae--Juvenile literature. 2. Amphibians--Juvenile literature. I. Title. II. Series: Solway, Andrew. Adapted for success.
  QL668.E233S65 2006
  597.87'7--dc22
                        2006014294

Acknowledgments
The author and publisher are grateful to the following for permission to reproduce copyright material:
Alamy pp. 29, 37 (Blickwinkel) 30, 36 (Bruce Coleman INC.), 38 (Papilio); Corbis pp. 33 (Michael & Patricia Fogden), 25 (Tom Brakefield); DK Images pp. 4, 27, 42 (right), pp. 42 (left) (Colin Keates), 6 (PhotoDisc/Harcourt); FLPA pp. 31 (Minden), 23 (Minden/Fogden); Getty Images pp. 39 (National Geographic), 6 (PhotoDisc), 35 (Stone), 24, 26 (Taxi); Jose Luis Gomez de Franciso p. 20; NHPA pp. 11 (A.N.T. Photo Library), 16 (Daniel Heuclin), 32 (Stephen Dalton); Nick Garbutt p. 21; OSF pp. 28 (David M Dennis), 41 (Kathie Atkinson), 13 (Michael Fogden); Science Photo Library pp. 17 (Adam Hart-Davis), 22 (Art Wolfe), 15, 34, 43 (Claude Nuridsany & Marie Perennou), 40 (Dan Suzio), 12 (David Aubrey), 14 (Gary Meszaros), 10 (Mark Smith), 18 (Martin Dohrn); Stephen M Deban and Nature Magazine p. 19.

Cover photograph of strawberry poison frog with chin extended reproduced with permission of NHPA/ George Bernard.

The publishers would like to thank Ann Fullick for her assistance in the preparation of this book.

Contents

Some words are shown in bold, **like this**. You can find out what they mean by looking in the glossary.

Introduction to Adaptation

Poison frogs are colorful residents of the Amazon rainforests. Most frogs hide away by day and are active at night to avoid **predators**. However, poison frogs are active by day. Their bright colors should make poison frogs easy targets for predators, but few predators would try to eat one. The most poisonous **species** has enough toxin (poison) in its skin to kill 10 people or 20,000 mice.

In water and on land

Poison frogs are **amphibians**—animals that live part of their life in water and part on land. Amphibians have thin skins that easily lose water, so they must live in moist conditions to avoid drying out. They are **cold-blooded**, which means that they rely on the environment for heating and cooling. They cannot keep their bodies at a constant temperature the way birds and **mammals** do. However, amphibians have managed to **adapt** to living in nearly all parts of the world, from hot deserts to cold climates.

The golden poison frog is probably the most toxic of all the poison frogs.

A successful group

Amphibians are a very successful group of **vertebrates**, but what does it mean for an animal to be successful? One indication that amphibians are successful is that they have been around for a long time. The earliest fossil frogs are about 230 million years old. But amphibians are thought to go back further than this. Their earliest ancestors were animals called tetrapods that lived about 375 million years ago. Tetrapods were the first vertebrates to move out of the ocean and onto land.

Another measure of the success of a group is the number of species in that group. There are more species of amphibians than there are of mammals—5,399 amphibian species compared with 4,680 mammal species. By this measure, amphibians are very successful.

Adapting in many ways

When the first amphibians moved onto land 375 million years ago, there were very few species. As amphibians spread into new areas, and began to live in different ways, they had to adapt to survive. Different **adaptations** gave rise to different species. Today, after millions of years, the thousands of different amphibians on Earth have evolved (changed gradually over time).

Frogs begin life as eggs and then become tadpoles, which usually live in water and breathe through **gills**. Gradually the tadpoles develop legs and lungs.

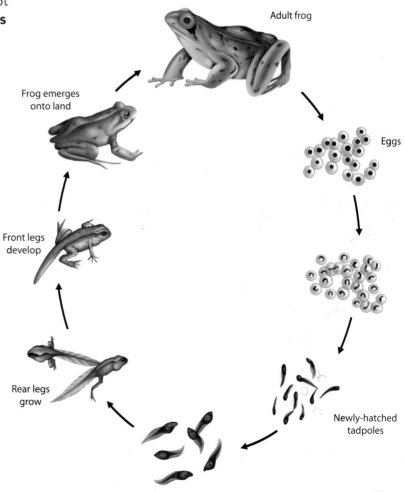

Adult frog

Frog emerges onto land

Eggs

Front legs develop

Rear legs grow

Newly-hatched tadpoles

How Does Adaptation Work?

How have amphibians adapted to fit into so many different environments? **Evolution** is the process by which life on Earth has developed and changed. Life first appeared on Earth 3.5 billion years ago. Since then, living things have evolved from simple single **cells** to the estimated 10 million or more different species on Earth today.

The frogs and newts in this pond are not in **direct competition** because they eat different foods. This is why both species can live together in the same **habitat**.

Useful changes

Adaptation is an important part of evolution. Adaptations are ways in which a living thing changes to fit into a particular environment and way of life. For instance, a pond frog's webbed feet are an adaptation to help it swim, while a poison frog's toxic skin is an adaptation that keeps away predators so it can feed during the day.

Amphibians do not choose their adaptations. They are the result of **variation** and **natural selection**.

Variation

Not all individuals of the same species are exactly the same. You can see this yourself if you look around your class at school. Some people are taller than others. Some people have light hair, while others have dark hair. Some people are musical, and some are good at sports. These differences between individuals of a species are known as variations.

ALL IN THE GENES

Living things pass on characteristics to their offspring through their **genes**. A living thing's genetic material is a kind of instruction book for that individual.

Most animals and plants produce offspring by sexual reproduction. Males and females each produce special cells, known as **gametes**, which have only half the normal genetic material. Each parent provides half the genetic information for their offspring.

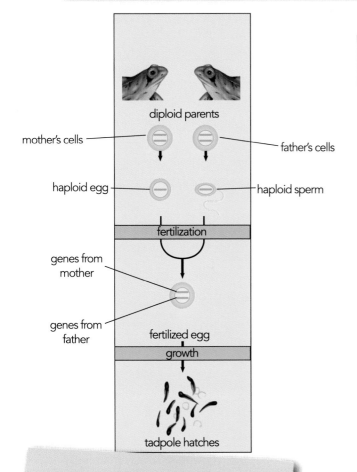

diploid parents

mother's cells

father's cells

haploid egg

haploid sperm

fertilization

genes from mother

genes from father

fertilized egg

growth

tadpole hatches

This diagram shows the process of amphibian reproduction. Each parent produces gametes (egg cells and sperm cells) that are haploid. They have only half the normal genetic material. When the gametes combine, they form a **fertilized** egg with a full set of genes.

Natural selection

Variation among individuals is what makes it possible for a species to change and adapt. The driving force for adaptation is called natural selection.

In any environment, there is a limited number of food sources. Different species compete with each other for food, for space, and for **mates**. The animals that are most successful at getting food and space to live are able to grow and **reproduce**. They pass on their useful characteristics to their **offspring**.

If animals move into a new environment, or if there are changes in their environment, natural selection will help the species adapt. For example, when frogs began to live in forests, the frogs with toe pads that allowed them to climb vertical surfaces were most successful, so a completely new species of frogs with specialized toe pads evolved.

More About Amphibians

Modern amphibians are divided into three broad groups. The biggest group are the frogs and toads. There are 4,750 frogs and toads, which is over 85 percent of all amphibians. The other groups are salamanders and a small, little-known group of amphibians called caecilians.

HOW DO YOU TELL A FROG FROM A TOAD?

In Europe and North America, frogs are smooth-skinned, live around water or in trees, and have teeth. Toads are heavy-bodied, warty, and have no teeth. However, African clawed toads are smooth-skinned and live in water, and many squat, warty toads are called frogs. In fact, there are no clear differences between frogs and toads. *Frog* and *toad* are just different names for the same type of animal.

Frogs and toads

The basic body plan of frogs and toads is similar in all species. All frogs and toads have a short body with a rigid spine, and no obvious tail. Their back legs are long and powerful, adapted for leaping. Frogs and toads have large eyes and they rely heavily on sight for finding food. Nearly all frogs are predators.

Frogs have lungs for breathing air, but the lungs are very simple structures. A frog cannot get enough oxygen to survive by its lungs alone. Instead, a frog **absorbs** much of the oxygen it needs through its thin skin (see pages 10–11). This happens both in water and on land, but the skin must be kept moist for the process to work.

Salamanders and newts

Salamanders and newts make up about 10 percent of all amphibians, or around 470 species. They look more like lizards than frogs, with a long, flexible body and a long tail. Unlike lizards, however, salamanders breathe through their skin, like frogs. They also lay eggs with a jelly-like coating, while lizards' eggs have shells.

Some salamanders live mainly on land, some live mainly in the water, and some live part of the time on land and part in water. Many species that live mainly in water have fish-like gills to help them breathe.

Caecilians

Caecilians are a small group of amphibians that look like worms. There are just 176 known species of caecilians. Their bodies are divided into segments like a worm, but they have a backbone and other body parts like amphibians. Caecilians are burrowing animals, and live either in soil or in the bottoms of lakes and rivers. They feed on beetles, worms, termites, and other soil animals.

Metamorphosis

The larvae of most amphibians are different from the adults. Frog and toad larvae are called tadpoles. They have gills for breathing underwater and long tails for swimming. Tadpoles feed mostly on water plants. As they grow, tadpoles gradually develop legs and lose their gills and tail. These changes are called **metamorphosis**.

Having a different larval stage is an adaptation that allows frogs and toads to live in different habitats and feed in different ways when they are larvae. In this way, the larvae do not compete with adults for food and space.

Newt and salamander larvae are not so different from adults, while caecilian young look like small adults.

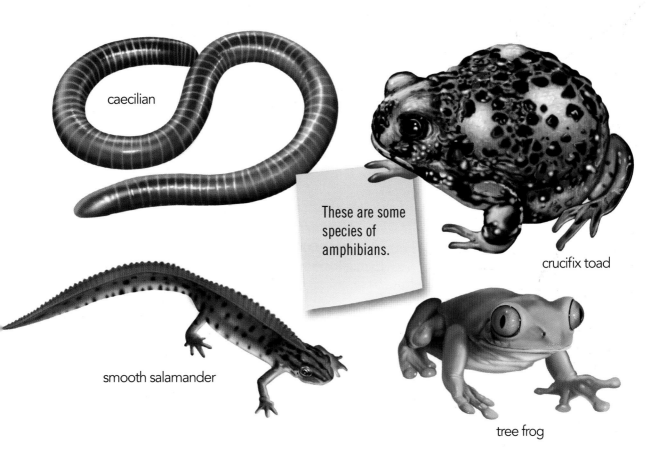

caecilian

These are some species of amphibians.

crucifix toad

smooth salamander

tree frog

Amphibian *Skin*

All animals get energy from their food by breaking it down into simpler substances, such as carbon dioxide and water. Oxygen is an essential part of this process. Animals need it in order to get energy to survive and grow.

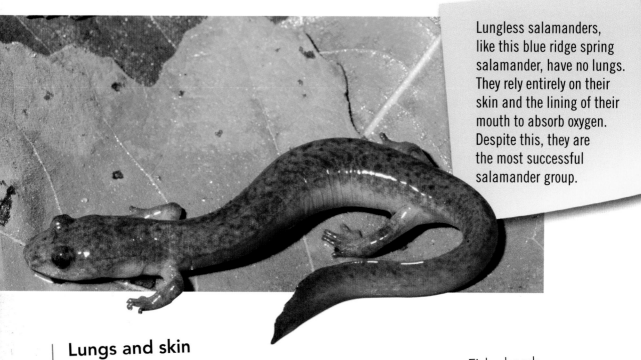

Lungless salamanders, like this blue ridge spring salamander, have no lungs. They rely entirely on their skin and the lining of their mouth to absorb oxygen. Despite this, they are the most successful salamander group.

Lungs and skin

Water contains oxygen, and about 25 percent of air is oxygen. Fish absorb oxygen from water through their gills, while most land vertebrates have lungs to get oxygen from air. Amphibians have lungs, like other land animals, but they also absorb oxygen through their skin.

In order to work as an extra lung, an amphibian's skin has to be thin and moist. As well as letting oxygen in, this thin skin lets **water vapor** out. This means that when it is on land, an amphibian is constantly losing water to the air.

Different environments

Because amphibians need to keep their skin moist, and because they are cold-blooded, most amphibian species live in warm, moist areas such as rainforests. Frogs in particular are abundant in rainforests. There are 90 frog species at one rainforest site in Ecuador, almost the same number as in all of North America.

The water-holding frog, seen here inside a waterproof cocoon, lives in the dry deserts of southern Australia. It spends most of its life buried underground, coming out only after it rains to mate.

In many tropical climates there is a dry season and a rainy season. During the very dry conditions of the dry season, some amphibians lie **dormant** underground and are only active in the rainy season. This is called **aestivation,** and it is similar to hibernation. Australian water-holding frogs guard against water loss by burrowing underground and then encasing themselves in a cocoon of **mucus**. The mucus hardens to form a shell around the frog that prevents water loss.

Many amphibians have special patches of skin that are very good at taking up water from damp soil. This helps them replace the water they lose on land.

GLANDS IN THE SKIN

Amphibians have many **glands** in their skin, some of which produce mucus to cut down on water loss. Other glands produce poison. In poison frogs, the poison glands produce more powerful toxins than in other amphibians. Some species are so poisonous that even touching them can kill a person. Some native peoples of the Amazon rainforest use the poison from these frogs to coat the tips of their hunting darts and arrows.

Adaptations to Different Habitats

The earliest amphibians looked very much like modern salamanders, with long bodies, long tails, and fairly short legs. However, amphibians also have evolved another body shape, which allows them to take advantage of many more habitats. Frogs and toads all have short bodies, no tail, and long back legs.

More than 80 percent of all frog species live in the tropics. By contrast, most salamanders live in **temperate** areas, although some salamander species live in the tropical rainforests of Central and South America.

Trees and water

Some frog species that live in tropical forests are adapted for climbing. Tree frogs are small, with long legs and large sucker-like toe pads that help them cling onto branches, twigs, and plant stems. A few salamander species that live in the forests of Central and South America have **prehensile** tails to give them a better grip when climbing.

Very few frogs spend their whole lives in water, but several groups of salamanders are **aquatic** for their entire lives. Some aquatic salamanders have adapted to living in water by keeping the feathery gills seen in larvae, and they have tiny legs or no legs at all.

Like other tree-living species, this red-eyed tree frog has sucker-like toe pads that help it grip and climb.

Cooler climates

In temperate areas, most amphibians live near ponds and streams so they have constant access to water. At colder times of the year they become torpid (inactive) because their bodies are too cold for the muscles to work.

Most amphibians can survive long periods at temperatures just above freezing. Some species, such as the wood frog of North America and the European common frog, can survive temperatures as low as -21 °F (-6 °C). They can survive at these temperatures because their blood contains about 100 times more glucose than normal, which works as a kind of antifreeze.

FLYING FROGS

Some tree frogs in Southeast Asia have evolved a quick and efficient way of moving around the forest. They have huge webbed hands and feet, and webbing down the sides of their bodies. The frogs jump from branch to branch with their hands and feet spread out, and the large areas of webbing allow them to glide from tree to tree.

A flying frog spreads its large webbed feet as it makes a gliding leap from one tree branch to another.

Going underground

The worm-like caecilians are well adapted for living underground. Their long, thin, smooth shape is ideal for burrowing. Caecilians dig their way through the soil with their head. They have adapted to digging this way by developing thick, strong skull bones. Their skin is firmly attached to the skull bones, to stop it from being pulled away during digging.

Other amphibians also dig burrows. Some frogs live in areas where the weather is dry for part of the year. Many of these frogs have adapted to these conditions by burrowing underground during the dry season. Spade-foot toads dig burrows with their back feet. They have a hard-edged digging tool on each back foot. Shovel-nosed frogs dig their burrows head first. They have pointed snouts adapted for digging.

Poisonous Predators

Nearly all adult amphibians, including poison frogs, are predators. Many of them feed on insects, spiders, worms, and other small **invertebrates**.

A North American green frog eats a dragonfly. Green frogs are unusual because they hunt for food both by day and by night.

Daytime hunters

Poison frogs are unusual among amphibians because they feed during the day. Most amphibians hunt at night or underground because this keeps them out of sight from their many predators. However, the poison frogs' **toxic** skin means that they have few worries about predators and can afford to hunt by day. They are very active feeders, and are always on the move. Their main **prey** is ants and termites, but they also feed on any other small creatures they find.

Eyes and tongue

Like other frogs and toads, poison frogs rely mainly on sight to find their prey. They have large eyes on the top of their head that give them good all-round vision. A poison frog's eyes are better adapted to daytime vision than those of other frogs. Despite their bright colors, poison frogs probably cannot see colors themselves. It is their predators, particularly birds, that recognize the frogs' bright colors and learn to avoid them.

Poison frogs catch prey using their tongue. The tongue is attached to the mouth at the front instead of at the back. It is long and has a sticky pad on the end. When an insect or other prey comes close, the poison frog flips its tongue out of its mouth and catches the victim on the sticky end of its tongue. Many other kinds of frog and toad catch prey in the same way.

Poisonous food

The natural diet of a poison frog includes many ants and mites. These creatures have toxic chemicals in their bodies, which help make the frogs' skin poisonous. Before the toxic chemicals are carried to the skin, they are modified inside the frog's body to become even more poisonous.

Poison frogs kept in zoos or as pets often lose their skin poisons because there are no ants and mites in their diet.

Some mantella frogs from Madagascar have poisonous skin and bright colors, like the poison frogs of South America. This is an example of **convergent evolution** (see box below).

CONVERGENT EVOLUTION

Some poison frog species in the rainforests of Madagascar (off the coast of Africa) have bright colors and toxic skin chemicals similar to those found in South American poison frogs. Although the frog species are similar, they are not closely related. Both groups of frogs have independently evolved similar sets of adaptations to protect them from predators. The evolution of similar characteristics in animals that are not related to each other but live in similar habitats is known as convergent evolution.

Feeding Adaptations in Other Amphibians

Nearly all amphibians are **carnivores**. They eat insects, spiders, and other small creatures. However, many amphibian larvae feed on plants. Most frog and toad tadpoles eat plant food or filter small food particles from the water. This means that they can live in different environments from the adults and do not compete directly with them for food and space.

Night hunters

Most frogs and toads are sit-and-wait predators. They are also **nocturnal**. During the day, they hide under logs or in shallow burrows to avoid predators and hot weather.

Most frogs eat small creatures such as insects and spiders. They are not usually fussy eaters and catch anything that comes their way. A few large frogs, such as the American bullfrog, eat birds, mice, snakes, fish, and sometimes smaller frogs. Many frogs rely on their excellent eyesight to spot prey. However, Central American burrowing toads also have a good sense of smell, which they use to sniff out underground termite tunnels.

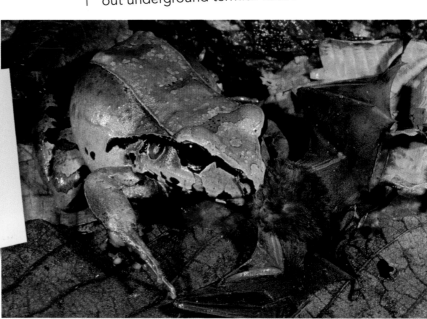

Knudsen's frog is a large species that lives in the Amazon region. It is capable of killing small animals such as this bat.

Flippers and snappers

Most frogs flip out their tongue straight in front of them to catch prey. However, the red-banded rubber frog can flip out its tongue in almost any direction. This enables it to catch prey to one side of, or even slightly behind, its head.

Not all frogs catch their food by flipping out their tongue. Some frogs and toads have short tongues and catch their prey by snapping it up in their mouth.

Small appetites

Being cold-blooded has advantages when it comes to feeding. Amphibians and other cold-blooded animals do not need as much food as **warm-blooded** animals of a similar size. This is because warm-blooded animals use a lot of energy keeping their bodies warmer than their surroundings.

When conditions for tadpoles become crowded, and there is not enough food to go around, they sometimes become cannibals (see box below).

CANNIBAL TADPOLES

Tadpoles are usually plant-eaters or **filter feeders**. However, if the food supply gets low or the tadpoles' pool starts to dry up, they can suddenly change their diet and start eating each other. Although it sounds strange, this kind of cannibalism is actually an adaptation to difficult conditions. If a pool dries up before the tadpoles complete their metamorphosis into frogs, all of the tadpoles will die. By eating each other, some of the tadpoles have a chance of survival.

Salamanders Feeding

Most salamanders are predators and, like frogs and toads, they eat mainly insects and other small animals.

The palmate newt lives most of its life in water. Fish such as the stickleback are a major part of its diet.

Finding prey

Salamanders usually hunt at night, like frogs and toads. A salamander's eyesight is much poorer than that of a frog, but its eyes are good at sensing movement. When there is enough light, salamanders use their eyes to spot the movement of their prey. Salamanders also have very good senses of smell and taste, which they can use to track prey in the dark.

In the water, smell and taste are not useful senses for tracking prey. Salamanders that hunt in water rely on their eyes to pick up prey movement. They also have another sense organ called a lateral line organ, which picks up slow vibrations in the water. These are the kinds of vibrations made by fish and other water creatures while swimming.

Catching prey

Salamanders eat all kinds of small prey, including insects, spiders, worms, snails, and centipedes. Those that feed in water often prey on frog tadpoles. Some larger species of salamander, such as spring salamanders and giant salamanders, catch larger prey, including fish, crabs, other salamanders, and small snakes.

Most salamanders that hunt on land are sit-and-wait predators. Like frogs and toads, many salamanders have a sticky tongue for catching prey. Many lungless salamanders have an extra-long tongue that they can shoot out suddenly to catch insect prey. Salamanders have small teeth in both upper and lower jaws and in the roof of the mouth. These teeth are adapted to hold prey and to stop them from escaping once inside the mouth.

QUICK ON THE DRAW

Salamanders hold the world record for quick-draw tongues. Some miniature salamanders can shoot out their tongue, catch a prey animal, and retract the tongue again within the space of just 6 milliseconds! This is over 10 times faster than any frog, and nearly 100 times faster than the much larger chameleon.

Salamanders that hunt underwater do not have a long tongue, as this would be useless underwater. These species catch their food in a way that is similar to some fish. They have a wide mouth, which they open suddenly when a prey animal comes close. When the mouth opens, water rushes in, sucking the prey animal in with it.

Unlike tadpoles, salamander larvae are predators. They also have normal teeth like adults, whereas frog and toad tadpoles have only hardened ridges in their mouths.

A salamander can extend its tongue up to half its body length in order to catch food.

Camouflage Coloring

An important part of being a successful sit-and-wait hunter is being hard to spot. Many amphibians have excellent **camouflage** that allows them to blend in with their environment.

Uses of camouflage

Camouflage is an important adaptation that helps amphibians hide from their enemies. It can also help hide an amphibian from its prey. For this reason sit-and-wait hunters that hunt during the daytime are usually well camouflaged. Camouflage does not help night-hunting species hunt, but it can be an important way to stay hidden during the day.

The patterns and shades of a camouflaged animal can also serve a completely different purpose. They make it possible for animals of the same species to recognize each other. This can be important during the **mating season**, when animals are looking for a mate.

The colors and patterning of the marbled salamander help it blend in with its surroundings.

Changing color

Many amphibians can change their color to suit their background. This adaptation greatly improves their camouflage. A frog in a shady area will become darker in color, while a frog in bright sunlight will become lighter.

As well as being good camouflage, changing color helps a frog keep its temperature steady. Dark colors absorb heat, so in the shade a dark frog can absorb more heat from its surroundings. In contrast, light colors reflect heat and light, so being light-colored in the sun helps reflect excess heat.

An Asian horned toad sitting among the dead leaves of the forest floor is very hard to see.

Camouflage masters

Some amphibians have developed especially good camouflage. The Asian horned toad is a large sit-and-wait predator that lives among **leaf litter** on the forest floor in Southeast Asia. Its skin color and patterning match the dead leaves around it. Its body is also flattened and it has horns over each eye, which make its shape like that of a dead leaf. It even has veins on its skin that look like the veins on a leaf. The frog uses this excellent camouflage to help it catch insects and smaller frogs.

Vietnamese mossy frogs also are masters at camouflage. These frogs live along the banks of mountain streams, where mosses and other small plants grow in large numbers. The skin of a mossy frog has a collection of bumps, spines, and other sticking-out parts that make it look like a clump of moss. These frogs hunt at night and use their amazing camouflage to hide from enemies during the day.

HIDDEN COLORS

Scientists have discovered that some frogs change their color to suit their **infrared** background. This probably helps them hide from monkeys and even pit vipers, which have sensitive heat-sensing organs.

Warning Colors

Poison frogs do not have camouflage colors. In fact, they have the opposite. They are brightly colored and stand out against their background. The frogs' bright colors serve as a warning to predators that they are poisonous. Several other amphibian species also use bright warning colors in this way.

The bright yellow-and-black markings of this yellow-banded poison frog act as a warning signal to predators.

A common language

All kinds of poisonous or unpleasant-tasting animals, from insects to skunks, have warning colors. These warning colors are usually a combination of a bright color, or white, with black. Birds and other predators learn that animals with these colors are bad to eat, and so they avoid them.

Several other kinds of amphibians have warning colors like poison frogs. The mantella frogs in Madagascar have bright colors similar to those of poison frogs. Harlequin frogs of Central America and the corroboree frog of Australia are also poisonous, and both of them have vivid black-and-colored patterns on their skin. Many salamanders also have poisonous skin and bright colors. Fire salamanders have bold patterns in yellow and black, while mud salamanders are a vivid red.

Brightly colored fakes

Not all brightly colored amphibians are poisonous. A few harmless species have also adapted bright colors and patterns very similar to those of another poisonous amphibian. Because they look like the poisonous species, predators also avoid eating them, even though they are, in fact, harmless. One example is the eastern red-backed salamander of North America. This harmless salamander looks very similar to the larva of the red-spotted newt, which has poisons in its skin that are deadly to predators.

DEFENSE AGAINST POISON

Although poison frogs are deadly to humans and to most predators, each species seems to have at least one predator that is immune to, or not badly affected by, the poison. The fire-bellied snake, for example, regularly attacks and eats poison frogs. It even eats golden poison frogs, which are the most poisonous of all frogs.

All predators and prey are constantly involved in a struggle to survive. As a predator evolves adaptations for catching and killing prey, the prey animals evolve defenses against their predators. In the case of poison frogs, the toxins in their skin are an effective defense against most predators. However, at least one predator has become immune to the frogs' poison, and others will probably do so as well. As predators become more successful at catching and killing poison frogs, the frogs will need to evolve new defenses against them or they will die out.

A fire-bellied snake swallows a poisonous harlequin frog in Costa Rica.

23

Jumping Frogs

If you have ever tried to get close to a frog, you will know that it is not easy. If the frog is near water, it will disappear below the surface in one leap. Otherwise, it will make a series of zigzag leaps, each one heading in a different direction, before disappearing into long grass or some other kind of cover. Leaping is the most important defense against danger for many species of frog.

Adapted for leaping

A frog's long back legs, its stiff backbone, and the lack of a tail are all adaptations for leaping. The long legs give more leverage (push) from the ground, while the lack of a tail gives the legs more space to move and cuts down on weight and drag. The front legs also need to be strong to absorb the impact of landing.

Leaping on land and in water

Although leaping has had a major influence on how all frogs look, quite a few frogs no longer leap. Large, heavy frogs, for instance, hop rather than leap, and there are a few frog species that do not leap at all.

Frogs that live mainly in trees climb with a walking action, moving one leg at a time. When they want to move from one branch to another, however, they leap like frogs on the ground. In the water, frogs swim by kicking out both legs at the same time and then drawing them together. This swimming movement is similar to the leaping action.

The long back legs of the red-eyed tree frog are adapted for leaping from branch to branch in the trees.

When a frog swims it uses a similar leg action to a human swimming the breaststroke, as this picture of an African clawed frog shows.

FROGS' LEGS

The European frog *Rana esculenta* and the smoky jungle frogs of Central and South America are excellent leapers with strong back legs. However, their leaping ability has got them into trouble. *Rana esculenta* are better known as edible frogs because their legs are a great delicacy (special dish), especially in France. Smoky jungle frogs are called mountain chicken in the Caribbean because their leg meat is so delicious.

An unknown mechanism

Leaping is a useful adaptation, both for escaping from enemies and for suddenly attacking prey. Either or both of these benefits might have been the reason why frogs developed into leaping animals. However, scientists have no hard evidence to show what the **evolutionary force** was that led frogs and toads to adapt in this way. There are two main scientific theories:

- Frogs evolved the kicking action as a way of swimming in water and later adapted to leaping on land.
- Leaping began on land and was later adapted for swimming.

Frog Defenses

Frogs have a huge range of enemies. Many snakes live almost entirely on frogs, and birds such as herons are expert frog-catchers in shallow water. Turtles attack frogs in the water, while bats snatch frogs from trees. Smaller frogs may be eaten by larger frogs, and tadpoles are food for almost any water predator. To survive among so many enemies, frogs need a wide range of defenses.

The bold markings on the sides of a red-eyed tree frog suddenly appear as it leaps. This sudden ash of color can startle a predator.

Startling defenses

Some frog species use camouflage and others have poisonous skin to defend themselves against predators. Many frogs also leap away from danger. However, some frogs have evolved a further defense mechanism to startle enemies when they jump. The red-eyed tree frog is mostly bright green, but it has bright blue markings along its sides and on its legs. When the frog is at rest, the markings are hidden. When the frog jumps, the markings appear as a sudden flash of color, then disappear again as the frog lands. The sudden flash confuses the predator for a second, and this gives the frog a few moments to escape.

Some other tree frogs have a brightly colored tongue, which they show when threatened. This may startle an attacker in a similar way to flash markings. Fire-bellied toads have dull-colored back and sides, but if they are threatened, they lift up their head and legs to show a bright red or orange and black belly.

FOUR-EYED DEFENSE

The false-eyed or four-eyed frog has two large, dark spots on its back end. When it is threatened, the four-eyed frog drops its head to hide its eyes and lifts up its back end. The attacker sees two large eyes in what looks like the head of a larger animal. If the display does not scare off the attacker, the frog has a further trick up its sleeve. The eyespots are actually poison glands that can squirt a poison spray at any enemy that gets too close.

Staying put

Rather than running away, some frogs and toads stay put when threatened. Some species freeze while others play dead. Toads often puff up with air to make themselves look bigger. Budgett's frog, from South America, puffs up with air, arches its back, opens its huge mouth, and screams like a cat in pain.

Some toads can do more than just puff themselves up and scream. Like other toads, cane toads rise up and puff themselves up when first threatened. If the threat continues, they squirt their attacker with a spray of poison from glands on the head.

When threatened, the false-eyes frog of South America hides its head and shows the false eyes on its back end.

Salamander Defenses

Salamanders and newts are small, soft-bodied creatures that cannot leap to escape their enemies. Yet they have adapted to survive, despite having enemies ranging from birds of prey to centipedes.

Quiet and hidden

One of a salamander's main defenses against predators is to be shy and secretive. Salamanders usually stay hidden during the day— hiding under logs, in rock crevices, in burrows, or anywhere else that is moist and dark. They come out to feed at night, but quickly return to hiding if they sense any threat.

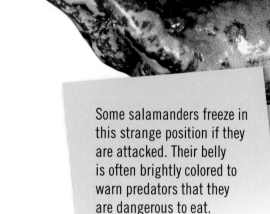

Some salamanders freeze in this strange position if they are attacked. Their belly is often brightly colored to warn predators that they are dangerous to eat.

Poison skin

If a predator sees a salamander, there are other defenses that it can use. A salamander's skin is full of glands that produce slippery mucus, which make it hard to hold, and unpleasant or poisonous liquids. Both of these are effective ways to scare off an attacker.

Some mole salamanders have poison glands on the back of the head. When they are attacked, they lower their head and headbutt their enemy. Other salamanders, such as the tiger salamander, have poison glands in their tail. When it is attacked, the tiger salamander uses its powerful tail to slap its attacker in the face. The tail glands release poisonous liquids that make the slap much more unpleasant.

Some lungless salamanders, such as the cave salamander, also have poison glands in their tail. However, the tail is not powerful enough to lash an attacker. Instead, the cave salamander hides its head and waves its tail around. The waving tail attracts the predator's attention, leaving the head safe from attack. If the predator grabs the tail it gets a mouthful of horrible secretions. As a last resort, the salamander can actually shed its tail and escape.

CHEMICAL WARFARE

Although salamanders have poisons in their skin, they are not completely safe from predators. For each salamander poison, there is usually at least one snake that is immune to it. As fast as new poisons evolve in the salamanders, snakes also evolve to become immune to the poisons.

The fire salamander's bright colors and markings warn predators that it is poisonous.

Sprays and ribs

Fire salamanders have effective defenses in their skin. Along the middle of its back are giant poison glands that can spray out a jet of poison. The fire salamander can aim the spray and hit a target up to 13 feet (4 meters) away. The spray can cause painful burning in human eyes, and even temporary blindness.

Sharp-ribbed salamanders and spiny newts have glands in their tails like many other species. However, they have one further line of defense. If they are bitten, their rib bones stick through the skin and prick the inside of the predator's mouth. The ends of the ribs are sharp and, in the salamander, they poke out through poison glands. This means that many poison-tipped bones prick the predator's mouth.

Poison Frog Social Life

Poison frogs live in the leaf litter on the rainforest floor. Most of the time, they live and hunt alone. However, during the mating season, males and females work together to reproduce and bring up offspring.

The posion frog parent, usually the father, carries the tadpole on its back. The tadpole is held there by sticky mucus that stops it from falling off.

Courtship and mating

At the start of the mating season, male poison frogs compete with each other for **territories**, areas of the forest that have good sites for laying eggs. Once a male has a territory, he begins to make trilling or buzzing calls to attract a female. If he manages to attract a female, the frogs stroke each other during a courtship ritual. In some species, the courtship involves males and females wrestling with each other.

Once a male and female have paired up, the female lays her eggs and the male deposits sperm to fertilize them. Usually the female lays her eggs in a hidden place close to water.

Eggs and tadpoles

In some species of poison frog, the male guards the fertilized eggs, while in other species the female also helps guard them. The parent or parents check the eggs regularly to make sure they are moist. When the eggs hatch, one of the parents (in most species, the male) carries the newly hatched tadpoles, one at a time, to places where they can grow and develop into frogs. Good places might be small pools, water caught in the hollow of a tree, or rainwater caught in a **bromeliad** or other plant.

In some poison frog species, the tadpoles are left to fend for themselves at this point. In other species, however, the tadpoles are often put in pools where there is nothing to eat. To make sure the young survive, the female frog travels regularly to each tadpole pool and lays unfertilized eggs in the water. These eggs are the tadpoles' main food.

Poison frog eggs take about two weeks to hatch, and the tadpoles take ten to twelve weeks to mature into frogs. A female poison frog, therefore, may be looking after her offspring for fourteen weeks before they can fend for themselves. Poison frogs take about two years to fully mature and be ready to reproduce. They may live for up to ten years.

FERTILIZING THE EGGS

Like most frogs and toads, male poison frogs fertilize the female's eggs as she lays them. To do this, the male rides around on the female's back, clinging onto her using special horny pads on his front feet. As the female lays each egg, the male covers it with sperm.

A strawberry poison dart frog mother deposits tadpoles one by one into pools of water in rainforest plants. She will scatter them among the trees to give them a higher chance of survival.

Many Kinds of Reproduction

Poison frogs are not typical of amphibians in the way they reproduce. Most species return to the water to mate and lay large numbers of eggs. This is not the only way that amphibians reproduce, however. There are more different kinds of reproduction among amphibians than in any other vertebrate group.

Female frogs lay between 6 and 25,000 eggs.

Frogs and toads

Most frogs and toads reproduce by external fertilization. This is when a female frog's eggs are fertilized outside her body. In most frog species, this happens in the same way as it does for poison frogs. The male rides around on the back of the female and deposits sperm on each egg that she lays.

A few frog species reproduce by internal fertilization. This means that the male places sperm inside the female's body, and the eggs are fertilized there.

Laying eggs

Most female frogs lay hundreds or thousands of eggs. Each egg has a thin layer of jelly, which expands in water to form a protective coating. One of the parents may guard the eggs until they hatch, but otherwise they get no parental care. Many of the eggs and tadpoles die before they develop into frogs. A few frog species are like the poison frogs—they lay fewer eggs but, by looking after them, they ensure that most survive.

In a few amphibians, the eggs do not hatch into tadpoles but into miniature adults because the tadpole or larva stage happens inside the egg. This kind of development is an adaptation by species that live in dry conditions.

Salamanders and caecilians

A few salamanders reproduce by external fertilization, like frogs and toads. However, most salamanders and all caecilians reproduce by internal fertilization. Most salamanders and newts transfer sperm from the male to the female in a packet called a **spermatophore**. The male lays the packet on the ground, then leads the female to the right position to pick up the sperm. The female then takes the spermatophore into her body to fertilize the eggs.

NO MALE GENES

In some North American mole salamanders, the female's eggs contain a full set of the mother's genes. A male's sperm is needed to start the eggs developing, but none of the male's genes go into the egg. The offspring are clones of their mother. In this form of reproduction, no males are produced. The males that supply the sperm to start egg development belong to a closely related salamander species.

After mating, most salamanders lay fertilized eggs. In a few salamander species and half of caecilians, however, the eggs develop inside the female and are born as small versions of the adults. One or two frog species, such as the African live-bearing toad, also produce live young.

This is an adult caecilian. Young caecilians can take up to eleven months to develop inside the female. During this time, the young feed on milk inside the female's body.

Frog Choruses

Male poison frogs attract females by calling. Other male frogs and toads make calls to defend their territory and to attract a partner. Some frog species gather in large groups to mate. In other species, females are more selective about which male they choose to mate with.

Quick or slow

Frogs mate and breed in two different ways. Frogs such as American wood frogs and European common toads are known as explosive breeders. This means the males gather in large groups at breeding ponds, and their calling attracts large numbers of females. Mating takes place over just a few nights, and then the breeding season is over. Studies have shown that in frogs that breed explosively, there is less cannibalism among the tadpoles (see page 17) because they are all the same age and size.

Other frogs have much longer mating seasons, which last up to six months. Each night some males come to breeding ponds and call, but not every male comes every night. Each night of calling attracts just a few females, so only a few males get to mate every night.

Making a noise

Frog calls range from croaks and buzzes to trills and whistles. When a frog or toad calls, it blows up balloon-like sacs in its throat or cheeks. These are called vocal sacs. The air in the vocal sac helps amplify the sound.

This male edible frog is calling. As well as attracting mates, the calls mean that a male has claimed that territory.

In warm parts of the world, where there are many frog species, most areas of water have a frog chorus every night during the breeding season. In these choruses, several different species call at the same time, each trying to attract a female. The call of each species has its own particular sound. In some cases, scientists have been able to separate two frog species that look very similar by listening to the calls they make.

Picking the right mate

The calls of different species cannot overlap too much or the females will not be able to tell them apart and mating will not take place. Females recognize the calls of their own species because their hearing is adapted to be especially sensitive to those calls.

In species that breed explosively, there are roughly as many males as females at any breeding site, and females have little chance to choose mates. However, in prolonged breeders, only a few females arrive at a breeding site each night, and they usually have many males to choose from. Studies show that females usually choose to mate with the males that call longest and most often. Calling takes a lot of energy so males that make long, frequent calls are probably stronger and more likely to produce strong offspring.

LOUD CALLERS

The calls of some frogs species, such as the American bullfrog, can carry more than 0.6 miles (1 kilometer). The flute-like calls of the Barbados whistling frog are not so loud, but they are more impressive because the frogs are only about 0.8 inches (2 centimeters) long!

Looking After the Young

Most amphibians give their eggs little care beyond choosing a good egg-laying site. Quite a few species, however, do give their eggs some care. Some, such as poison frogs, also care for the larvae once they are hatched.

Caecilians and salamanders

Around half of all caecilians give birth to live young. In caecilians that lay eggs, the female protects the eggs by lying coiled around them while they develop.

Many salamanders lay their eggs in water, but a few lay them on land. Salamanders that lay their eggs on land usually produce 20 to 30 eggs. They lay them in a damp place such as the middle of a rotting log. Often the parents guard the eggs while they are developing.

Salamanders that lay their eggs in water lay up to 500 eggs. In the water, the eggs usually receive no care once they have been laid.

Foamy nests

Most frogs and toads lay their eggs in water and give them little care. However, many forest species lay their eggs on land. Since the jelly-like coating around amphibian eggs is not waterproof, the eggs need to be kept moist to stop them from drying out. Different frog and toad species have developed different adaptations to achieve this.

Many tree frogs protect their eggs in a nest of foam. The frogs make the foam by using their legs to beat a liquid that the female produces. The outside of the foamy nest sets like meringue (dried egg whites), but the inside stays moist. Gray tree frogs make these foam nests in groups. The nests have to be over pools of water so that the tadpoles can drop into the water when they hatch. Sites of this sort are probably quite rare. That might be why whole groups of frogs lay their eggs together.

Female gray tree frogs lay their eggs in a tree and produce a liquid. The males beat this liquid with their legs to form a foam nest.

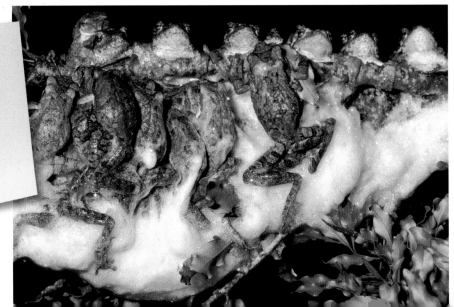

A group of male midwife toads carry eggs.

Backpacking

Some frogs care for their eggs by carrying them around. Male midwife toads carry strings of eggs wrapped around their legs, while marsupial frogs carry their eggs in a pouch on their back. Both these adaptations give the eggs a much better chance of survival. However, the parents have to invest more time and energy in their offspring, which means that they can breed less often.

A few species care for their offspring when they are tadpoles. In marsupial frogs the young do not leave the mother's pouch until they are fully developed froglets. South African toad tadpoles are born in shallow pools that disappear quickly in the dry season. The male toad makes sure that the tadpoles have enough water by digging channels from one pool to another.

HARD TO SWALLOW

Australian gastric frogs care for their young in an odd way. Once the eggs have been fertilized, the female frog swallows them and they develop inside her stomach. When they are big enough, the baby frogs hop out of their mother's mouth!

Disappearing Amphibians

Around the world, scientists have noticed a large decrease in the number of many amphibian species. Pollution, diseases, hunting for food, and habitat loss all may be reasons for the rapid decline. Several species of amphibian are known to have become **extinct** in the past fifteen to twenty years.

Troubling losses

The declines in some amphibian species are troubling for several reasons. Some species in certain areas have almost disappeared within two or three years, but other species in the same area seem to be unaffected. Scientists do not understand why one species has been affected but not another. Another troubling discovery is that amphibians are disappearing even in national parks and nature reserves.

Loss of habitat

As with all other animals, loss of habitat is a major threat to amphibians. Marshes, swamps, ponds, and other kinds of wetland are ideal amphibian habitats, but they are disappearing fast. Many kinds of wetland have been drained and turned into farmland or cleared for buildings.

One amphibian species that has been affected by habitat loss is the blue poison frog. It is found only in small, forested areas on the island of Surinam, and many of these forested areas have been cut down. The blue poison frog is now critically endangered and is likely to become extinct in the wild.

The blue poison frog is highly vulnerable to both illegal collecting and natural factors, such as drought, due to its extremely small **range** and isolated (spread far apart) populations.

Early warning

Amphibians seem to be more badly affected than other animals by the effects of pollution and damage to the environment. The disastrous declines in amphibian numbers may be an early warning of similar declines in other kinds of animal.

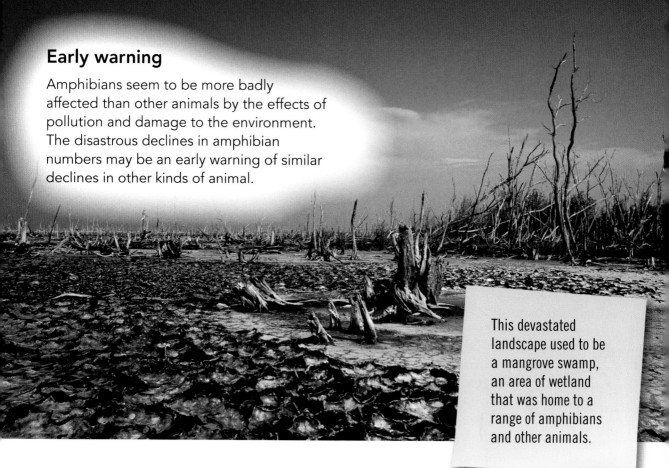

This devastated landscape used to be a mangrove swamp, an area of wetland that was home to a range of amphibians and other animals.

Pollution and disease

Research has uncovered many possible causes for the decline in amphibians. One cause is pollution. Chemicals such as artificial fertilizers and **pesticides** that are sprayed on farm crops get washed into water where amphibians live. Amphibians are badly affected by chemical pollution because the chemicals are easily absorbed through their thin skin. Scientists think that the red-legged frog, which was once common along the West Coast of North America, has been badly affected by one pollutant—nitrates.

Disease is another cause of amphibian decline. One especially bad disease caused by a fungus eats away at a frog's skin. This disease is thought to have wiped out the tinkling frog, which was found only in a small part of Queensland, Australia. It also has affected amphibians in Central America and the eastern United States.

GOLDEN TOADS

Golden toads were discovered in 1969 in the Monteverde cloud forests of Costa Rica. Their numbers began to drop in the 1970s, and in 1989 only one frog was found in the yearly check on their numbers. Since then no golden toads have been seen, and they are thought to be extinct. Recent evidence suggests that global warming has caused their disappearance. Since the 1970s, the forests have been covered by clouds less and less often because of the overall warming of the climate.

Unfair Competition

A few amphibians have done well in man-made environments after humans have introduced them into new areas. However, some of these species have had serious effects on the **native** amphibians in the area.

American bullfrogs have become a pest in many areas where they have been introduced by humans.

American bullfrogs

American bullfrogs are large, adaptable predators with a huge appetite and the ability to spread quickly in new areas. They were originally found in the southeast of the United States, but they have spread to other parts of the United States and Canada, where they are farmed for frogs' legs. In these areas, bullfrogs have competed against local frogs and toads so successfully that the local species are dying out. American bullfrogs have also spread to parts of Europe, where they are kept for food and as pets. Conservationists are trying to get rid of bullfrogs in many areas, to stop local frog species from being wiped out completely.

Cane toads

Cane toads are native to Central and South America, where they were known as marine or Mexican toads. They are large toads that have poison glands on either side of their head. They can squirt an attacker with poisonous liquid. Like American bullfrogs, they are fierce predators. They usually eat insects, but they also catch and eat small snakes, frogs, lizards, and even mice.

In 1935, 100 cane toads were introduced into Australia. It was hoped that the toads would eat insects and other creatures that were damaging sugar cane crops. However, the toads did not stay in the sugar cane plantations because there was nowhere for them to hide during the daytime. Instead, they moved into the surrounding countryside and into people's gardens. With no natural predators, the number of cane toads increased rapidly. Conservationists are worried that the toads are eating many local amphibian species and seriously affecting their numbers.

Generalists and specialists

Cane toads and American bullfrogs are examples of successful amphibians. They are **generalists** that live in a wide range of environments and eat all kinds of food. They rapidly adapt to the conditions in new environments. Many other amphibians, however, cannot adapt quickly enough to the rapid changes caused by humans. The species that are most at risk are **specialists** that have adapted to a specific kind of habitat or live on a certain kind of food.

A cane toad devours one of the native Australian frog species.

PROTECTING AMPHIBIANS

Although the numbers of many amphibians are falling, conservationists have had small successes in protecting and encouraging some amphibians. In Europe and North America, road signs and special tunnels under the roads have saved the lives of many frogs and toads returning to their home ponds to breed. Encouraging farmers and gardeners to create small ponds has also helped amphibian populations. Another success has been with disease in amphibians. Conservationists have cured amphibians that have fungal disease using medicines designed to treat

Extinct Amphibians

Since the first amphibians appeared 375 million years ago, many species have appeared, flourished, and then become extinct. It is not known exactly why many of these animals died out. Some may have become extinct because of changes in the climate, which has changed many times in the millions of years since amphibians first appeared. Other amphibians may have died out because of competition from species that were better adapted to the environment.

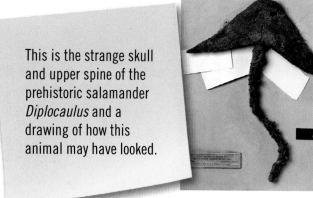

This is the strange skull and upper spine of the prehistoric salamander *Diplocaulus* and a drawing of how this animal may have looked.

The age of the amphibians

From about 350 to 300 million years ago, amphibians were very successful. There were so many species that this period is sometimes called the Age of the Amphibians. One group of amphibians that was successful at this time was the temnospondyls. There were many different species. Some species lived in the water, and others lived partly in the water and partly on land. The largest were about ten feet (three meters) long and were like amphibian versions of crocodiles.

Over the next 50 million years or so, the climate got hotter and drier. This did not suit amphibians, and early reptiles became the **dominant** land animals. However, some temnospondyls survived in water until about 160 million years ago.

Other amphibians from around the same time as temnospondyls looked more like modern salamanders. *Diplocaulus* was about the size of a large modern salamander (about 39 inches, or 1 meter) and had a long body and short legs. However, its wide head was a very strange triangular shape. Scientists have various theories about its strange head. It may have helped *Diplocaulus* to glide through the water, or it may have been a defense adaptation that made it difficult for predators to swallow its head.

Modern amphibians

Modern amphibians arose from a group of small, long-bodied, land-living amphibians similar to modern salamanders. This happened between 305 and 240 million years ago. However, the earliest fossil salamander is from much later than this—about 150 million years ago. Fossil frogs of about the same age have been found in North Korea.

Some frogs and salamanders living today look very similar to the fossil amphibians from 150 million years ago. If humans can protect more habitats and learn to live with amphibians, rather than destroying them, these amphibian species may still be living on Earth in 150 million years.

FISHY ANCESTORS

The first amphibians evolved from a group of fish known as lobe-finned fish. These fish had strong fins that they used to pull themselves along. They also had simple lungs, similar to those of lungfish today. Although they are not closely related to lungfish, these ancestors of the first land animals may have lived in a similar way. Lungfish live in shallow water or swamps, and they often move along the bottom by pulling themselves along with their fins. One kind of modern lungfish, the South American lungfish, has small gills and can breathe only in air.

Fish similar to this South American lungfish may have been the early ancestors of amphibians.

Further Information

Amazing amphibian facts

Biggest amphibian	Chinese giant salamander	Can grow up to 5 ft. 11 in. (1.8 m) and weigh 143 lb. (665 kg)
Biggest frog	West African goliath frog	Grows to about 1 ft. (30 cm) long
Smallest frog	Cuban leaf litter frog	Only about 0.4 in. (1 cm) long
Coolest frog	North American wood frog	Survives as far north as the Arctic and spends 2–3 months each year frozen
Longest living frog	European common toad	One toad is known to have lived to 40 years old
Longest jump	South American sharp-nosed frog	At a frog derby in South Africa in 1977, a frog named Santjie jumped over 33 ft. 6 in. (10 m)

Amphibian classification

Family	Number of species	Description/distribution
Caecilians		
6 families	176	Worm-like, with segmented body, between 2.8 in. (7 cm) and 5 ft. 2 in. (1.6 m) in length
Salamanders		
10 families. Largest three families are:	470	
Lungless salamanders	266+	Typical-looking salamanders found in woodland, caves, or mountain streams in southern and western United States and Central and South America
Newts and European salamanders	55+	Mostly land species, breed in ponds; found across Europe, parts of China, and the eastern United States
Asiatic salamanders	35+	Mostly land species, breed in ponds; found across eastern Russia and in parts of China

Frogs and toads		
28 families. Largest are:	4,750	
Leptodactylid frogs	864	Diverse group of frogs found throughout South and Central America
Amero-Australian tree frogs	777	Mostly live in forests in South America and Australia, but also in Europe and East Asia
True frogs	643	Very diverse group of frogs, found worldwide; includes American bullfrog, edible frog, wood frog, and goliath frog
Narrow-mouthed frogs	414	Mostly land-living or digging frogs; found in forests and grasslands in tropical areas
True toads, harlequin frogs, and relatives	378	Mostly land-living frogs and toads; found on all continents; include European common toad and cane toad

Books

- Behler, John L., and Deborah A. Behler. *Frogs: A Chorus of Colors*. New York: Sterling, 2005.
  – This book showcases the 5,000 species of frogs, from the tiny Brazilian flea frog to the African goliath frog

- Beltz, Ellin. *Frogs: Inside Their Remarkable World*. Buffalo, NY: Firefly Books, 2005.
  – This book covers all families of frogs, with lots of information about adaptation and the environment

- Hofrichter, Robert, ed. *Amphibians: The World of Frogs, Toads, Salamanders, and Newts*. New York: Firefly Books, 2000.
  – This encyclopedia provides coverage of over 4,800 recognized varieties of amphibian, including frogs, toads, newts, and salamanders

Websites

- Exploratorium museum, San Francisco
  www.exploratorium.edu/frogs/mainstory/index.html
  – Information and activities about frogs

- American Museum of Natural History
  www.amnh.org/exhibitions/frogs
  – Facts and fun about frogs

Glossary

absorb take in or soak up, like a sponge

adapt when a living thing changes to fit in with its environment

adaptation change that helps a living thing fit into its environment

aestivation sleeping through the hot, dry summer

amphibian animal with smooth skin that lays eggs in a jelly-coating and usually spends part of its life in water and part on land

aquatic able to live in water

bromeliad plant with stiff, wiry leaves forming a cup that catches and holds water

camouflage coloring and patterning that help an animal hide from its enemies or blend into the background

carnivore meat-eating animal

cell tiny building block of all living things

cold-blooded animal that cannot keep its body temperature constant and relies on the environment to heat or cool it

convergent evolution evolution of similar characteristics in animals that are not related to each other but live in similar habitats

direct competition when two species of living things live in the same habitat and eat the same foods. Eventually one species will become dominant and the other will become extinct.

dominant most important

dormant alive but not growing

evolution process by which life on Earth has developed and changed

evolutionary force something that makes a group of animals begin to evolve and change, such as a change in the climate or a food source becoming scarce

extinct when all animals of a certain species die out

fertilize when a sperm cell combines with an egg cell to form the first cell of a new living thing

filter feeder living thing that gets food by straining small creatures or tiny pieces of food from water

gamete male or female sex cell, usually sperm or egg

generalist living thing that can live in a variety of habitats

gene something that is transferred from a parent to its offspring that determines some features of that offspring

gill breathing organ found in some aquatic amphibians that helps them breathe underwater

gland part of the body that produces some kind of liquid

habitat place where an animal lives

infrared kind of light below the red end of the spectrum (rainbow), that humans cannot see but feel as heat

invertebrate animal without a backbone

larva (plural larvae) the young of insects, spiders, frogs, and some other animals

leaf litter layer of dead and rotting leaves on the floor of a forest

mammal warm-blooded, usually furry animal that feeds its young on milk

mate animal's breeding partner; also, when a male and female animal come together to produce young

mating season time of year when courtship and mating take place

metamorphosis stage in an animal's life cycle when a larva changes into an adult

mucus thick, sticky liquid produced by the lining of some parts of an animal's body

native animal that belongs to an area

natural selection mechanism of evolution by which only those individuals that are best fitted to their habitat and lifestyle survive and reproduce

nocturnal animal that hunts only at night

offspring young of an animal

pesticide chemical that is used to kill insects, spiders, or other small creatures that feed on farm crops

predator animal that hunts and kills other animals for food

prehensile having a tail that can grip

prey animal that is eaten by a predator

range places where a living thing is known to live

reproduce produce young

specialist living thing that is adapted to a particular habitat

species group of very similar animals that can breed together to produce healthy young

spermatophore packet of sperm produced by a male amphibian

temperate climate with mild temperatures

territory area that animals defend against other animals of the same species

toxic poisonous

variation difference among individuals within a species

vertebrate animal with a backbone such as mammals, birds, reptiles, and amphibians

warm-blooded able to keep the body at a constant temperature

water vapor water as a gas

Index